Satan,
You Lying Devil, You!

Satan, You Lying Devil, You!

Lannie Richmond

Fresh Ink Group
Roanoke

Satan,
You Lying Devil, You!

Copyright © 2016
by Lannie Richmond
All rights reserved

Fresh Ink Group
An Imprint of:
The Fresh Ink Group, LLC
PO Box 525
Roanoke, TX 76262
Email: info@FreshInkGroup.com
www.FreshInkGroup.com

Edition 1.1   2016

Book design by Ann Stewart/FIG
Cover design by Stephen Geez/FIG
Art by Anik/FIG

Scripture quotations marked NIV are from the Holy Bible New International Version © 1973, 1978, 1984, 2011 by Biblica, Inc. Used by permission. All rights reserved.

Scripture quotations marked NJKV are from the Holy Bible, New King James Version Copyright © 1982 by Thomas Nelson, Inc.

Scripture quotations marked KJV are from the King James Version of the Bible.

Scripture quotations marked NLT are from the Holy Bible, New Living Translation, Copyright © 1996, 2004, 2007 by Tyndale House Foundation. Used by permission of Tyndale House Publishers, Inc., Carol Stream Illinois 60188. All rights reserved.

Some names of persons mentioned in this book have been changed to protect privacy; any similarity between individuals described in this book to individuals known to readers is purely coincidental.

Except as permitted under the U.S. Copyright Act of 1976, no part of this publication may be reproduced, distributed, or transmitted in any form or by any means, or stored in a database or retrieval system, without prior written permission of the publisher.

Cataloging-in-Publication Recommendations:
REL006000 RELIGION / Biblical Studies / General
REL006050 RELIGION / Biblical Commentary / General
REL095000 RELIGION / Christian Education / Adult

Library of Congress Control Number: 2016962937
Paper-cover ISBN-13: 978-1-936442-47-8
Hardcover ISBN-13: 978-1-936442-46-1
Ebook ISBN-13: 978-1-936442-48-5

Dedication

*This book, my second,
is dedicated to my wonderful wife
of more than 34 years,
Lori.*

*We acknowledge Jesus
as our Lord and Savior of all mankind.
Thank you, Jesus.*

Contact

If you would like to contact
Lannie and Lori Richmond
for speaking engagements in your church,
we can be reached by writing to

**In His Light Ministries
PO Box 255
Dewitt, Michigan 48820**

Table of Contents

Chapter 1	Satan Begins His Lying Ways	1
Chapter 2	Satan's Lies Didn't Affect Jesus	15
Chapter 3	Satan and People	29
Chapter 4	Satan Is Man's Enemy	57
Chapter 5	Satan Focuses on Our Weakness	75
Chapter 6	Jesus	87
	The Prayer for Salvation	94
	Salvation	95

Chapter 1
Satan Begins His Lying Ways

Satan has a plan that always has some kind of a lie attached to it, making you think he is on your side to help you or to show you happiness. Listening to him causes you to sin, and sin always has a mess with it. It hurts you and others, and it robs happiness. Satan was shrewd. He saw his chance to make a mess and start sin that would rob us of the happiness God brings.

Eve was the first woman created, which tells us a lot about the workings of Satan.

> *The serpent was the shrewdest of all the wild animals the Lord God had made. One day he asked the woman, "Did God really say you must not eat the fruit from any of the trees in the garden?"*
> —GENESIS 3:1 (NLT)

Satan was a liar from the start. Satan was out to put doubt in Eve by asking her a question that would make her start to doubt what God meant. God did not say she could not eat from any of the trees of the garden. God said that Adam and Eve could eat from every tree except the tree of the knowledge of good and evil.

> *But the Lord God warned him, "You may freely eat the fruit of every tree in the garden—*
>
> *except the tree of the knowledge of good and evil. If you eat its fruit, you are sure to die."*
>
> —GENESIS 2:16-17 (NLT)

Eve went out every day and knew she had the freedom of eating from every tree. She did not give a thought to the tree of the knowledge of good and evil. She was happy and had everything she needed and wanted. Satan cannot stand for anyone to be happy, so he asked her a question to make her think and doubt her happiness and freedom. He wanted her to think about that tree of the knowledge of good and evil.

> *"Of course we may eat fruit from the trees in the garden," the woman replied.*
>
> *"It's only the fruit from the tree in the middle of the garden that we are not allowed to eat." God said, "You must not eat it or even touch it; if you do, you will die."'*
>
> —GENESIS 3:2-3 (NLT)

Eve answered back with the truth of what God said. What Satan knew is while she was saying the truth of what God said he was lying to get her to doubt the real truth and deceive her to believe that he knew the real truth. She was speaking the truth of what God said, but in her mind she began to think about the tree that she was told not to eat or even touch. Satan knew he had her listening and could continue their conversation to make her believe his lies.

> *"You won't die!" the serpent replied to the woman.*
>
> *"God knows that your eyes will be opened as soon as you eat it, and you will be like God, knowing both good and evil."*

> *The woman was convinced. She saw that the tree was beautiful and its fruit looked delicious, and she wanted the wisdom it would give her. So she took some of the fruit and ate it. Then she gave some to her husband, who was with her, and he ate it, too.*
>
> —GENESIS 3:4-6 (NLT)

Eve was convinced. She looked at the tree she was not supposed to touch or eat from, and she saw that it was beautiful. She had a choice to believe God or Satan, and when she listened to Satan the serpent she chose not to believe God because her focus was on the very thing that God said to stay away from. The lies led her to believe Satan, and that tree was the very tree that showed her evil. It brought shame and every form of evil that we still have in this earth today.

THE DESTRUCTION OF CAIN & ABEL

> *Now Adam had sexual relations with his wife, Eve, and she became pregnant. When she gave birth to Cain, she said, "With the Lord's help, I have produced a man!"*
>
> *Later she gave birth to his brother and named him Abel. When they grew up, Abel became a shepherd, while Cain cultivated the ground.*

> *When it was time for the harvest, Cain presented some of his crops as a gift to the Lord.*
>
> *Abel also brought a gift—the best portions of the firstborn of his flock. The Lord accepted Abel and his gift,*
>
> *but he did not accept Cain and his gift. This made Cain very angry, and he looked dejected.*
>
> *—GENESIS 4:1-5 (NLT)*

Satan was at work; he knew he got Eve to believe him, and now he was going after Cain. Cain was a farmer and Satan was getting him to listen to him, so he didn't bring his best gift to God. Maybe he asked him a question or said something to him to make him believe it was better to keep the best for himself. Cain brought God more of what he didn't want for himself and was led to believe that this was great even though his heart was not in it. His heart was in the work that he did for the best gift he worked to produce. Abel brought the best but Cain listened to Satan and again did not pay any attention to God. God had a conversation with Cain, but Satan already had Cain's mind on believing lies so he would not give his best to God. If you believe God, you won't believe Satan. If you believe Satan, you won't believe God.

> *"Why are you so angry?" the Lord asked Cain. "Why do you look so dejected?*

"You will be accepted if you do what is right. But if you refuse to do what is right, then watch out! Sin is crouching at the door, eager to control you. But you must subdue it and be its master."

One day Cain suggested to his brother, "Let's go out into the fields." And while they were in the field, Cain attacked his brother, Abel, and killed him.

Afterward the Lord asked Cain, "Where is your brother? Where is Abel?"

"I don't know," Cain responded. "Am I my brother's guardian?"

But the Lord said, "What have you done? Listen! Your brother's blood cries out to me from the ground! Now you are cursed and banished from the ground, which has swallowed your brother's blood.

"No longer will the ground yield good crops for you, no matter how hard you work! From now on you will be a homeless wanderer on the earth."

Cain replied to the Lord, "My punishment is too great for me to bear!

"You have banished me from the land and from your presence; you have made me a homeless wanderer. Anyone who finds me will kill me!"

The Lord replied, "No, for I will give a sevenfold punishment to anyone who kills you." Then the Lord put a mark on Cain to warn anyone who might try to kill him.

So Cain left the Lord's presence and settled in the land of Nod, east of Eden.

—GENESIS 4:6-16 (NLT)

The ending is clear. Cain lost all that he held on to. The sin that Satan was setting up Cain to do brought him unhappiness and punishment. Satan did not do anything to help him but set him up to believe lies. Satan is not anyone's friend.

SATAN'S PLAN—GOD'S PLAN

Satan was succeeding to get people to believe lies, and this caused much sin. After sin comes punishment, so people had to sacrifice animals to be forgiven because the blood is what erases the sin causing destruction and bringing death to one's heart and life. Satan got that started when he tempted Eve. Men sacrificed animals so much because they sinned so much and needed the forgiveness from God. Satan knew if he worked his plan hard enough, he could wipe out animals. Then people would have no animals to sacrifice, and he could rule people with lies. There would be no forgiveness of sins. God is the creator, and He can create as much as He wants. God knew Satan's plan, so He came up with a plan He knew would permanently end the whole plan Satan had. When Jesus showed up on earth, Satan had a plan to kill him right from the start. Jesus was there, and that meant truth and his power were greater than Satan's. Satan from the beginning used power to try to deceive people into thinking lies were the truth. Satan was trying to use King Herod to kill the baby Jesus.

Jesus was born in Bethlehem in Judea, during the reign of King Herod. About that time some wise men from eastern lands arrived in Jerusalem, asking, "Where is the newborn king of the Jews? We saw his star as it rose, and we have come to worship him."

King Herod was deeply disturbed when he heard this, as was everyone in Jerusalem.

King Herod didn't want anyone to be worshipped but wanted all people to worship him. King Herod listened so much to Satan that Satan knew he could get King Herod to believe him and follow his plan.

—MATTHEW 2:2-3 (NLT)

Then Herod called for a private meeting with the wise men, and he learned from them the time when the star first appeared.

Then he told them, "Go to Bethlehem and search carefully for the child. And when you find him, come back and tell me so that I can go and worship him, too!"

—MATTHEW 2:7-8 (NLT)

King Herod had no intention to *worship* Jesus. I want you to pay close attention to the lie that Herod said to the wise men. He said find out and tell me *so that I can go and worship him.* It was no secret that Herod hated Jesus' birth, and now he was telling these very wise men entirely something else.

The wise men did not believe the lie, and they did not tell Herod where the child was. When you believe their lie, you receive a stamp of something robbing you of life and happiness. When you do like the wise men did, and know that the truth is greater, you will end up with happiness and blessing.

THE ESCAPE TO EGYPT

After the wise men were gone, an angel of the Lord appeared to Joseph in a dream. "Get up! Flee to Egypt with the child and his mother," the angel said. "Stay there until I tell you to return, because Herod is going to search for the child to kill him."

That night Joseph left for Egypt with the child and Mary, his mother,

and they stayed there until Herod's death. This fulfilled what the Lord had spoken through the prophet: "I called my Son out of Egypt."

Herod was furious when he realized that the wise men had outwitted him. He sent soldiers to kill all the boys in and around Bethlehem who were two years old and under, based on the wise men's report of the star's first appearance.

—MATTHEW 2:13-16 (NLT)

The first step was a lie. Herod never intended to worship Jesus. Satan never stops with a lie, but rather he continues to do one thing after another. However, the more you believe Satan's lies you will follow his plans.

JUDAS AGREES TO BETRAY JESUS

Then Judas Iscariot, one of the twelve disciples, went to the leading priests

and asked, "How much will you pay me to betray Jesus to you?" And they gave him thirty pieces of silver.

From that time on, Judas began looking for an opportunity to betray Jesus.

—MATTHEW 26:14-16 (NLT)

How many lies did Judas believe from Satan before he went to the leading priests and asked, how much will you pay me to betray Jesus to you? How many chances did Judas have to take hold of the truth and repent of the very thing that would defeat him? It did no damage to Jesus because Jesus is God and he is alive today. The damage of Judas Iscariot is told in *The Bible*.

JUDAS HANGS HIMSELF

Very early in the morning the leading priests and the elders of the people met again to lay plans for putting Jesus to death.

Then they bound him, led him away, and took him to Pilate, the Roman governor.

> *When Judas, who had betrayed him, realized that Jesus had been condemned to die, he was filled with remorse. So he took the thirty pieces of silver back to the leading priests and the elders.*
>
> *"I have sinned," he declared, "for I have betrayed an innocent man."*
>
> *"What do we care?" they retorted. "That's your problem."*
>
> *Then Judas threw the silver coins down in the Temple and went out and hanged himself.*
>
> —MATTHEW 27:1-5 (NLT)

Satan will entice you to sin and then condemn you for it just like he did with Judas. *Satan is a master of deception.* Judas never got the greatness or happiness with the money. The lie that Satan probably told Judas was that if he had the money, he would be rich and find the true happiness he always desired.

Satan works through people's thoughts. His battlefield is your mind. If he can get control of your mind, he can control your body. It's the very same scheme he used with Eve, Cain, and Judas. Satan worked at getting them to listen to him, and then he attacked their minds.

Satan is doing the same thing to attack people today. Satan is always after a person's mind. He puts thoughts in all our minds. Lies always start with a single thought.

Chapter 2
Satan's Lies
Didn't Affect Jesus

SATAN TEMPTED JESUS

Satan will usually try to get you in every way he can, and if nothing else works he will show up right at the time you feel the weakest. You might feel weak, but God's word, *The Bible*, is always your strength. Satan showed up to try to get Jesus to believe a lie and destroy God's plan, but think about what happened:

THE TEMPTATION OF JESUS

Then Jesus, full of the Holy Spirit, returned from the Jordan River. He was led by the Spirit in the wilderness,

where he was tempted by the devil for forty days. Jesus ate nothing all that time and became very hungry.

Then the devil said to him, "If you are the Son of God, tell this stone to become a loaf of bread."

But Jesus told him, "No! The Scriptures say, 'People do not live by bread alone'."

Then the devil took him up and revealed to him all the kingdoms of the world in a moment of time.

"I will give you the glory of these kingdoms and authority over them," the devil said, "Because they are mine to give to anyone I please.

I will give it all to you if you will worship me."

Jesus replied, "The Scriptures say,

'You must worship the LORD your God and serve only him.'"

Then the devil took him to Jerusalem, to the highest point of the Temple, and said, "If you are the Son of God, jump off! For the Scriptures say,

'He will order his angels to protect and guard you.

And they will hold you up with their hands so you won't even hurt your foot on a stone.'"

Jesus responded, "The Scriptures also say, 'You must not test the LORD your God.'"

When the devil had finished tempting Jesus, he left him until the next opportunity came.

—LUKE 4:1-13 (NLT)

I want for us to take a look at Satan and what he said and what he was trying to do to get Jesus to believe what he said. Jesus came from heaven and knew God face to face, so he knew all the truth and that there are no lies in heaven. Jesus is full of the truth. Satan wanted to get Jesus to listen to the lie enough so that he would receive the destruction of sin that goes along with the lie. That would destroy Jesus and cancel all of God's great plans. This would also deeply hurt God because Jesus is God's son.

Satan said to Jesus the words, "If you are the son of God." This is the same strategy he used with Eve. Satan tried to put doubt in Jesus' mind. Jesus did not doubt, though, because he knew God was his father and he trusted Him, and Jesus knew he was God's son. The truth of God's word was in him and he spoke it out. He said no. The truth, which is in *The Bible*, says you do not live by bread alone. Those words of truth were in Jesus. He did not have to stop and think for a second. He did not have to answer Satan's words or defend himself.

SATAN TRIES TO KILL JESUS

Satan tries to kill Jesus using people. Satan still tries today to get people to murder people.

> *At that point they picked up stones to throw at him. But Jesus was hidden from them and left the Temple.*
>
> —*JOHN 8:59 (NLT)*

Jesus was God, and no one could kill him until his appointed time. Satan knew Jesus had power, but he was going to try to trick him in hopes he could kill him. Satan loves death.

LIES AT JESUS' DEATH

Below are some verses that tell us about how Satan used people to tell lies about Jesus. Jesus knew Satan was behind all these lies. I want you to pay attention to Jesus' response.

> *Inside, the leading priests and the entire high council were trying to find witnesses who would lie about Jesus, so they could put him to death.*
>
> *But even though they found many who agreed to give false witness, they could not use anyone's testimony. Finally, two men came forward*
>
> *who declared, "This man said, 'I am able to destroy the Temple of God and rebuild it in three days.'"*
>
> *Then the high priest stood up and said to Jesus, "Well, aren't you going to answer these charges? What do you have to say for yourself?"*
>
> *But Jesus remained silent. Then the high priest said to him, "I demand in the name of the living God—tell us if you are the Messiah, the Son of God."*

> *Jesus replied, "You have said it. And in the future you will see the Son of Man seated in the place of power at God's right hand and coming on the clouds of heaven."*
>
> *Then the high priest tore his clothing to show his horror and said, "Blasphemy! Why do we need other witnesses? You have all heard his blasphemy.*
>
> *What is your verdict?"*
>
> *"Guilty!" they shouted. "He deserves to die!"*
>
> *Then they began to spit in Jesus' face and beat him with their fists. And some slapped him,*
>
> *jeering, "Prophesy to us, you Messiah! Who hit you that time?"*
>
> —MATTHEW 26:59-68 (NLT)

Jesus knew that Satan was using people to tell lies. Jesus knew God was in total control of this situation, and that his communication was with God, not Satan or people being used by Satan. Jesus knew everything that was going to happen was for a reason. It was to bring salvation and power to those who would later ask Jesus into their hearts. We can learn from Jesus' example, so when we are accused of something and we know people are lying, then we can remain silent and focus on God's plan. Our Father God can take care of the lies that come against us.

JESUS PREDICTS HIS DEATH

Then Jesus began to tell them that the Son of Man must suffer many terrible things and be rejected by the elders, the leading priests, and the teachers of religious law. He would be killed, but three days later he would raise from the dead.

—MARK 8:31 (NLT)

Jesus was talking to his disciples. This verse shows that Jesus knew the Father's will. Jesus knew what his purpose was and why he had to go through all he would go through. He would die for all the sins of the world.

THE SOLDIERS MOCK JESUS

The soldiers took Jesus into the courtyard of the governor's headquarters (called the Praetorium) and called out the entire regiment.

They dressed him in a purple robe, and they wove thorn branches into a crown and put it on his head.

Then they saluted him and taunted, "Hail! King of the Jews!"

And they struck him on the head with a reed stick, spit on him, and dropped to their knees in mock worship.

When they were finally tired of mocking him, they took off the purple robe and put his clothes on him again. Then they led him away to be crucified.

—MARK 15:16-20 (NLT)

THE CRUCIFIXION

A passerby named Simon, who was from Cyrene, was coming in from the countryside just then, and the soldiers forced him to carry Jesus' cross. (Simon was the father of Alexander and Rufus.)

And they brought Jesus to a place called Golgotha (which means "Place of the Skull").

They offered him wine drugged with myrrh, but he refused it.

Then the soldiers nailed him to the cross. They divided his clothes and threw dice to decide who would get each piece.

It was nine o'clock in the morning when they crucified him.

A sign announced the charge against him. It read, "The King of the Jews."

Two revolutionaries were crucified with him, one on his right and one on his left.

The people passing by shouted abuse, shaking their heads in mockery. "Ha! Look at you now!" they yelled at him. "You said you were going to destroy the Temple and rebuild it in three days.

Well then, save yourself and come down from the cross!"

The leading priests and teachers of religious law also mocked Jesus. "He saved others," they scoffed, "but he can't save himself!

Let this Messiah, this King of Israel, come down from the cross so we can see it and believe him!" Even the men who were crucified with Jesus ridiculed him.

—MARK 15:21-32 (NLT)

SATAN'S TOOLS

Satan's tools are fear, reasoning, doubt, deceiving, lying, and getting a person to have no concern for eternity. One of Satan's lies is to tell people they have plenty of time to get right with God. Satan uses fear to stop people from doing what God wants them to do. Fear is a Spirit. The ten men that were sent in to spy the Promised Land had fear of the people who lived there. Fear robbed them of ever getting into the Promised Land and receiving all that God had for them.

THE DEATH OF JESUS

At noon, darkness fell across the whole land until three o'clock.

Then at three o'clock Jesus called out with a loud voice, "Eloi, Eloi, lema sabachthani?" which means "My God, my God, why have you abandoned me?"

Some of the bystanders misunderstood and thought he was calling for the prophet Elijah.

One of them ran and filled a sponge with sour wine, holding it up to him on a reed stick so he could drink. "Wait!" he said. "Let's see whether Elijah comes to take him down!"

Then Jesus uttered another loud cry and breathed his last. And the curtain in the sanctuary of the Temple was torn in two, from top to bottom.

When the Roman officer who stood facing him saw how he had died, he exclaimed, "This man truly was the Son of God!"

Some women were there, watching from a distance, including Mary Magdalene, Mary (the mother of James the younger and of Joseph), and Salome.

They had been followers of Jesus and had cared for him while he was in Galilee. Many other women who had come with him to Jerusalem were also there.

—MARK 15:33-41 (NLT)

Jesus told her, "I am the resurrection and the life. Anyone who believes in me will live, even after dying.

—JOHN 11:25 (NLT)

Satan was in every plan in Jesus' death to try to destroy him. God knew and Jesus knew that everything that would be done to him would be for a reason, to free us and allow us to have power over the enemy Satan. Satan lied, tried to steal, and tried to kill; but Jesus, through everything he went through, defeated Satan. Jesus took the keys away from Satan.

I am the living one. I died, but look—I am alive forever and ever! And I hold the keys of death and the grave.

Jesus conquered hell so no one has to go there if they accept Jesus as their savior and ask him for the forgiveness of their sins.

—REVELATION 1:18 (NLT)

If you confess with your mouth that Jesus is lord and believe in your heart that God raised him from the dead, you will be saved.

For it is by believing in your heart that you are made right with God, and it is by confessing with your mouth that you are saved.

—ROMANS 10:9-10 (NLT)

Chapter 3
Satan and People

Satan hates *all* the people God has created. Satan hates the people whom he has successfully gotten to believe his lies and do his work. When they die and go to hell, they will see that Satan, whom they thought was their friend, had deceived them on this earth. They will experience Satan's demons, who will bash them against a wall and torture them, and they will know who the real Satan and his demons are—but it will be too late. Satan will give some people power on earth, but those people will not have any power in hell. Satan loves to deceive to get people into hell where his demons can torture them. Satan uses the power strategy.

> *"Jesus told them, If God were your father, you would love me, because I came to you from God. I am not here on my own, but he sent me."*
>
> *"Why can't you understand what I am saying? It's because you can't even hear me!*

> *For you are the children of your father the devil, and you love to do the evil things he does. He was a murderer from the beginning. He has always hated the truth, because there is no truth in him. When he lies, it is consistent with his character; for he is a liar and the father of lies.*
>
> *So when I tell the truth, you just naturally don't believe me!"*
>
> —JOHN 8:42-45 (NLT)

Satan uses his power to destroy churches.

Some of these same people are in church gatherings to seek power in the church, masking themselves, but their real fruit comes out. These same people work to get a crowd to go against their church, and to follow them away from the church that God has placed them with.

Satan uses the strategy of offense. I have seen this time after time. Many churches are forced to close down because most of their congregation has left them to follow someone who was once a leader they trusted in their very own church. Within a short time, this person they followed turns on them, or something happens to destroy the people who left.

If you follow Satan's plan, he will lead you away to pounce on you. You have great protection under an anointed pastor. I did not say a perfect pastor or a pastor who does everything right. I said an anointed pastor. People who cause problems for the pastor or church should never be in leadership.

> *Such people claim they know God, but they deny him by the way they live. They are detestable and disobedient, worthless for doing anything good.*
> —TITUS 1:16 (NLT)

Not always do people see the disobedient ways of people like this verse says until they draw people into their evil ways. People can act a lot and say the right words outside until a pastor trusts them. It takes a team. Pastors do not do wrong in wanting to believe the best. A group of people exists who are disobedient, attacking God's anointed pastors. Many times people use logic to explain their actions, trying to convince everyone they are doing right. If you are speaking evil of someone or joining someone in doing something against someone else, you are being disobedient.

What about a pastor who lives in sin?

If you go to a church and there is a pastor who is caught in adultery or has stolen money from a fund, go to someone who is a leader above him. Do not ever join a plan to embarrass or throw him to the curb with torment. There is a right way and a wrong way to handle situations like this.

People will gossip long after the pastor steps down, and if you join in you will be part of a church being destroyed. The blame goes to the pastor when really the blame is the gossipers. The pastor started something, but the pastor left and now it is your job to help build up the church again.

We are to be builders of the church, the body of Christ. Satan uses people to keep problems and sin going on and on. There are churches who are talking about pastors who are long gone ten years ago and are not listening to the pastor they have. These people are feeling good as they say that the pastor they have now is not as good as the pastor they had ten years ago. "He visited us at our house, and he always spent so much time with visitors. This pastor doesn't spend time with people." If you have a problem with this pastor, it is not wise to speak or write a letter to him. Either pray or ask God to help you follow his leading, and do not say one thing against the pastor. If someone asks you why you are unhappy, you can refuse to answer. "I will not speak against God's anointed or

God's church." Satan uses people to keep talk going to destroy churches. Be like David and don't let Satan pull you into sin. Don't allow Satan to use your mouth to destroy anything of God.

> *He said to his men, "The Lord forbids that I should do this to my Lord the king. I shouldn't attack the Lord's anointed one, for the Lord himself has chosen him.*
>
> —1 SAMUEL 24:6 (NLT)

David had the choice and chance to kill Saul. Many of his friends got mad because he did not kill Saul. David knew that God had his anointing on Saul even though Saul chose sin instead of walking in the anointing God gave him. David chose to walk in God's ways and not harm Saul because he knew Satan would love to destroy what God had anointed. David chose to partner with God and let God do things his way. Either you punish and watch Satan laugh and destroy, or you let God handle the punishment and raise you up and bless you because you choose his ways.

Satan is alive and well in churches trying to cause as much trouble as he can by getting people to think bad, then speak bad, and finally to take action. A group of people can do a lot of good, and a group of people can do a lot of bad. Don't be a participant in a group who wants to do bad. Pray and let God handle the one who needs correcting.

As a pastor I had trouble with a woman who kept telling me how great the other pastors were and how much more they did than me. In time I found out how much damage she did to some of the other pastors that were there. When I was pastor of that church I had an open vision where Jesus told me to tell those people to shut their mouths and keep their hands off his pastors. He told me to tell the people there if they see things wrong with the pastor they are to come to me in prayer and, if they are correct, I will tell my Holy Spirit to deal with my pastor there.

How does Satan even have a chance with good people? Isn't it only with bad people? Choices make the difference between you and God or you and Satan. It doesn't matter how good you think you are or how good others think you are. We Christians all have an enemy, and that is the devil who has no intentions of leaving us alone. *The devil hates God and hates all people. He is here to steal, kill, and destroy. The devil wants you in hell.*

TWELVE SCOUTS EXPLORE CANAAN

The Lord now said to Moses, "Send out men to explore the land of Canaan, the land I am giving to the Israelites.

Send one leader from each of the twelve ancestral tribes."

So Moses did as the Lord commanded him.
—NUMBERS 13:1-3 (NLT)

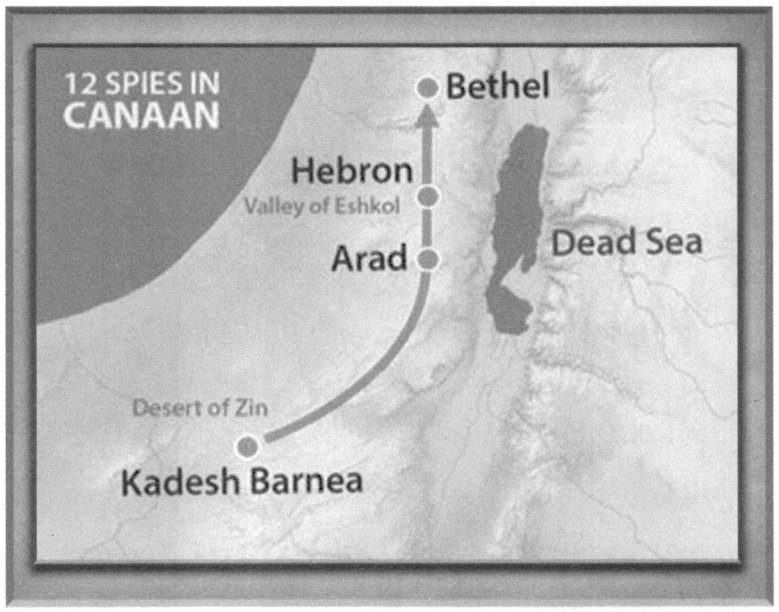

Moses gave the men these instructions as he sent them out to explore the land: "Go north through the Negev into the hill country.

See what the land is like, and find out whether the people living there are strong or weak, few or many.

See what kind of land they live in. Is it good or bad? Do their towns have walls, or are they unprotected like open camps?

Is the soil fertile or poor? Are there many trees? Do your best to bring back samples of the crops you see." (It happened to be the season for harvesting the first ripe grapes.)

—NUMBERS 13:17-20

This was their report to Moses: "We entered the land you sent us to explore, and it is indeed a bountiful country—a land flowing with milk and honey. Here is the kind of fruit it produces.

But the people living there are powerful, and their towns are large and fortified. We even saw giants there, the descendants of Anak!

But Caleb tried to quiet the people as they stood before Moses. "Let's go at once to take the land," he said. "We can certainly conquer it!"

But the other men who had explored the land with him disagreed. "We can't go up against them! They are stronger than we are!"

> *So they spread this bad report about the land among the Israelites: "The land we traveled through and explored will devour anyone who goes to live there. All the people we saw were huge.*
>
> *We even saw giants there, the descendants of Anak. Next to them we felt like grasshoppers, and that's what they thought, too!*
>
> —NUMBERS 13:27-33 (NIV)

Those two men, Joshua and Caleb, had no fear; and they got what God promised them. They entered into the Promised Land. Satan put thoughts in the mind of the ten spies. They had thoughts of fear. Satan defeated the ten when they gave into fear. Fear is a big tool that robs people today of getting the blessings that God wants to give. There have been surveys done with college students asking them what their biggest fear was. The top fear was public speaking.

There are many types of fear, including fear of the dark, fear of people, fear of failure, fear of marriage, etc. Fear can hold back happiness. Fear can paralyze people. I knew of a man who had a good job. His employer often required employees to give a small speech. He said he would quit his job if he was forced to speak in front of people. Many people give in to fear. We all feel fear, but we shouldn't let it control us. Just do it, even if you feel afraid! Fear is false evidence appearing real.

> *Fearing people is a dangerous trap,*
> *but trusting the Lord means safety.*
>
> *Many seek the ruler's favor,*
> *but justice comes from the Lord.*
>
> *The righteous despise the unjust;*
> *the wicked despise the godly.*
>
> —PROVERBS 29:25-27

REASONING

Reasoning is coming to conclusions without having the facts. Reasoning can become so real to people where they believe all their thoughts are true. Have you ever met someone who thought they were always right in everything they said because they knew it all? A know-it-all is not pleasant to be around. Reasoning has deceived him. He doesn't have the facts. The more a person uses reasoning, the more the devil will help and give you thoughts of reasoning. Remember that the devil is a liar.

There was a doctor who reasoned that people who were very ill needed assistance in dying quickly. He set up a way that quickly killed them. *The Bible* calls this murder. The doctor reasoned his act was good because the people were in pain and he was willing to help them get their wish. If those people who died were not saved, they are in worse torment than they were here on earth. You can reason all you want about death being better than living in pain, but I know the truth of death, of what happens when you die. My book called *Warning! No One Is scared of Hell Until They Get There* has my life story of how I went to hell. I will tell you the torment and fear are worse than anything anyone would experience on this earth. Your senses are very sharp in hell.

> *"But the fearful, and unbelieving, and the abominable, and murderers, and whoremongers, and sorcerers, and idolaters, and all liars, shall have their part in the lake which burneth with fire and brimstone: which is the second death."*
>
> —REVELATION 21:8 (KJV)

The second death is where your soul goes. That is who you are. In hell you are totally separated from God. The real life is on the inside of our body.

I had an aunt that I loved. I tried to talk to her about God and *The Bible*. She told me that she didn't believe *The Bible* and religion will drive you crazy. She said I haven't done any worse than anyone else. She died not knowing Jesus. She was very closed-minded when it came to anyone mentioning God. Reasoning closed her mind to the truth. She was a good person but *The Bible* doesn't say we get to heaven by being good. We all need to make Jesus our savior. Good people don't go to heaven; forgiven sinners go to heaven, and only Jesus can forgive sins.

I had a next-door neighbor whom I tried to talk to about Jesus. I tried to talk to him about accepting Jesus as his personal savior. He was very sick at that time. He told me that Jesus died for everybody so that everyone would go to heaven. He was wrong in his belief. He died shortly after that. Jesus did die for everyone's sins, but Jesus said you must be born again. You have to repent (turn away from sin to a life with God) and ask Jesus to forgive you of your sins. You must ask him to come into your heart and be your Lord and Savior. Without making Jesus your Savior you will go to hell.

> *Jesus saith unto him, I am the way, the truth, and the life: no man cometh unto the Father, but by me.*
>
> —JOHN 14:6 (KJV)

DOUBT

The dictionary's definition says doubt is to be uncertain about; consider questionable or unlikely; hesitate to believe, or to *distrust*. Doubting God means you don't have faith and trust in God.

> *But without faith it is impossible to please him: for he that cometh to God must believe that he is, and that he is a rewarder of them that diligently seek him.*
>
> —HEBREWS 11:6 (KJV)

Satan uses the tool of doubt to open the door to cause more destruction. Doubt leads to suspicion, and suspicion leads to not trusting God. Doubting your husband or wife can lead to jealousy, causing a breakdown between husband and wife. An extremely jealous person never can trust. Jealousy brings fighting and strife in a marriage.

Satan is here to destroy marriages. It is almost impossible to have a happy home, living with a person who is always questioning the spouse. "Where have you been? You're five minutes late getting home from work. Did you talk to anyone today? Who was that on the phone you were talking to?" Your spouse is always checking your phone for text messages. Many marriages go through this exact thing, some ending in divorce.

I had a grandfather who was so jealous he didn't allow his wife to answer the door. She had to leave the room if another man came into the house. People with jealousy imagine things in their minds. They are insecure in their relationships. Jealousy brings misery, and there is never any peace. A jealous person doesn't trust other people.

I don't like to be around jealous people. There is always a spirit of strife around them. A person never knows what they are thinking, or what they may do with a jealous mind. Many people have been killed because of the spirit of jealousy. Jealousy can lead to murder of an innocent person. A jealous mind is a confused mind. Jealousy ran big-time on my Father's side.

DECEIVING

The definition is to cause a person to believe what is not true; mislead or to catch by guile; ensnare. *The Bible* says that all liars will have their part in the lake of fire. Lying is a statement made to mislead or to deceive someone. A liar has the same character as Satan. *Satan is a master at deceiving people. There is no truth in Satan. Satan is the father of lies.* Deception is to believe a lie.

THE THOUSAND YEARS

> *And I saw an angel coming down out of heaven, having the key to the Abyss and holding in his hand a great chain.*
>
> *He seized the dragon, that ancient serpent, which is the devil, or Satan, and bound him for a thousand years. He threw him into the Abyss, and locked and*

sealed it over him, to keep him from deceiving the nations anymore until the thousand years were ended. After that, he must be set free for a short time.

—*REVELATION 20:1-2 (NIV)*

THE JUDGMENT OF SATAN

When the thousand years are over, Satan will be released from his prison

and will go out to deceive the nations in the four corners of the earth—Gog and Magog—and to gather them for battle. In number they are like the sand on the seashore.

They marched across the breadth of the earth and surrounded the camp of God's people, the city he loves. But fire came down from heaven and devoured them.

And the devil, which deceived them, was thrown into the lake of burning sulfur, where the beast and the false prophet had been thrown. They will be tormented day and night for ever and ever.

—*REVELATION 20:7-10 (NIV)*

Satan fights against Christians because he knows they belong to Jesus and can bring destruction to his evil kingdom of darkness. Christians can tell others about Jesus being the Savior of the whole world. Jesus is the only true

God. Satan hates Christians and uses government people of the world to try to stop Christianity from spreading. Jesus is the only door into heaven.

After we got married we both wanted to have a baby. My wife had some physical problems so we were unsure if she could get pregnant. We had been asking God for a baby. One night an audible voice from the outside whispered in my ear, saying tonight is the night you are going to get Lori pregnant. Later that night, my wife told me that God told her earlier that tonight she was going to get pregnant.

After we heard this voice, we believed it was God speaking to us, so we started telling everybody at our church. Every time we mentioned it to people that God had spoken to us and said that Lori was pregnant, she started her period. This went on for months. Lori went to the doctor and was told she was not pregnant. We got angered at God, and God spoke and said that was not me speaking to you. That was Satan talking to you. God said now that you stood the test, I am going to bless you with a baby. Right after that, Lori got pregnant and we had a baby boy.

Satan is still alive on earth today, and still lying and deceiving people. He is deceiving the governments of the world. He is using government people to pass sinful laws that God hates. Abortions are murder in God's eyes. Abortions end the life of a baby.

THE TEN COMMANDMENTS

Then God gave the people all these instructions:

"I am the Lord your God, who rescued you from the land of Egypt, the place of your slavery.

"You must not have any other god but me.

"You must not make for yourself an idol of any kind or an image of anything in the heavens or on the earth or in the sea.

You must not bow down to them or worship them, for I, the Lord your God, am a jealous God who will not tolerate your affection for any other gods. I lay the sins of the parents upon their children; the entire family is affected—even children in the third and fourth generations of those who reject me.

But I lavish unfailing love for a thousand generations on those who love me and obey my commands.

"You must not misuse the name of the Lord your God. The Lord will not let you go unpunished if you misuse his name.

"Remember to observe the Sabbath day by keeping it holy.

You have six days each week for your ordinary work,

but the seventh day is a Sabbath day of rest dedicated to the Lord your God. On that day no one in your household may do any work. This includes you, your sons and daughters, your male and female servants, your livestock, and any foreigners living among you.

For in six days the Lord made the heavens, the earth, the sea, and everything in them; but on the seventh day he rested. That is why the Lord blessed the Sabbath day and set it apart as holy.

"Honor your father and mother. Then you will live a long, full life in the land the Lord your God is giving you.

"You must not murder.

"You must not commit adultery.

"You must not steal.

"You must not testify falsely against your neighbor.

"You must not covet your neighbor's house. You must not covet your neighbor's wife, male or female servant, ox or donkey, or anything else that belongs to your neighbor."

—EXODUS 20:1-17 (NLT)

The United States government took the Ten Commandments out of schools and court houses. Tell me what's wrong with telling people they should not kill or steal, and to have respect for your mother and father. The United States government spends nothing on preventing crime, but billions of dollars each year on punishing criminals. Our prisons are filled with people who broke the Ten Commandments. Some may have never been taught the Ten Commandments. We hear our government talking about the increase in crime in our country and they say, What are we going to do about it? Their solutions are building more prisons and spending more money. Some day we may run out of money. Who pays for their ungodly solutions? You and I, the taxpayers, have to pay more taxes.

The United States has passed laws like gay marriage. Gays think they're married, but not in God's eyes.

The Bible says that homosexual lifestyle is an abomination to God. Abomination is an act that God is extremely against. Satan is behind gay lifestyles. He knows that living that lifestyle will lead them to hell. Only Jesus can set them free from the gay life.

> *So God abandoned them to do whatever shameful things their hearts desired. As a result, they did vile and degrading things with each other's bodies.*
>
> *They traded the truth about God for a lie. So they worshiped and served the things God created instead of the Creator himself, who is worthy of eternal praise! Amen.*
>
> *That is why God abandoned them to their shameful desires. Even the women turned against the natural way to have sex and instead indulged in sex with each other.*
>
> *And the men, instead of having normal sexual relations with women, burned with lust for each other. Men did shameful things with other men, and as a result of*

this sin, they suffered within themselves the penalty they deserved.

Since they thought it foolish to acknowledge God, he abandoned them to their foolish thinking and let them do things that should never be done.

Their lives became full of every kind of wickedness, sin, greed, hate, envy, murder, quarreling, deception, malicious behavior, and gossip.

They are backstabbers, haters of God, insolent, proud, and boastful. They invent new ways of sinning, and they disobey their parents.

They refuse to understand, break their promises, are heartless, and have no mercy.

They know God's justice requires that those who do these things deserve to die, yet they do them anyway. Worse yet, they encourage others to do them, too.

—ROMANS 1:24-32 (NLT)

But because you are stubborn and refuse to turn from your sin, you are storing up terrible punishment for yourself. For a day of anger is coming, when God's righteous judgment will be revealed.

He will judge everyone according to what they have done.

He will give eternal life to those who keep on doing good, seeking after the glory and honor and immortality that God offers.

But he will pour out his anger and wrath on those who live for themselves, who refuse to obey the truth and instead live lives of wickedness.

There will be trouble and calamity for everyone who keeps on doing what is evil—for the Jew first and also for the Gentile.

But there will be glory and honor and peace from God for all who do good—for the Jew first and also for the Gentile. For God does not show favoritism.

—ROMANS 2:5-11 (NLT)

SATAN, YOU LYING DEVIL, YOU

Satan tells people they're ugly, the're dumb, their lives won't amount to anything, that God hates them, they're not as good as other people and no one likes them, they can't do anything right. All of these are Satan's lies. God loves you and Satan hates you. Jesus is your friend. Lying Satan is your enemy. Satan is behind suicide people having no hope. Jesus is the hope of the whole world. Satan uses shame on people. Some people are ashamed of what they did when they were a child and Satan keeps reminding them of their past.

I saw a girl I went to elementary school with. She got pregnant as a young teen. We were both adults when I spoke with her. When I told her I remembered her by name she ran from me and it was obvious she was ashamed of her past. The past does not determine your future. Stay out of your past.

There is a popular singer whose music teacher told his mother that he can't sing at all. His mother didn't believe that lie and didn't give up on her son's singing. He went on and became a millionaire singing and recording music. God didn't create failures. If you listen to Satan's lies you will quit and become a failure. Satan uses depression, discouragement, and lack of confidence to hold people back. This is a major cause of suicides in America.

The United States was founded on God. The government was founded on God. *The Bible* was the book of laws. People in our government said that *The Bible* should be in each school. The Ten Commandments were posted in our schools and courthouses. *The Bible* was used in our courthouses as a book of oath. People were told to lay your right hand on *The Bible* and say, "Do you swear to tell the truth, the whole truth, nothing but the truth, so help you God?" *The Bible* was used in courts to honor the truth of God's word. *The Bible* is still God's truth.

> *Blessed is the nation whose God is the LORD; and the people whom he hath chosen for his own inheritance.*
>
> —*PSALM 33:12 (KJV)*

This used to be America until our government promoted all the evil sins in our country.

NO CONCERN FOR ETERNITY

Evil people came in and took *The Bible* out of schools and courthouses and removed The Ten Commandments. They made it unlawful to pray in school. Atheists say they don't believe in God, but they are offended if we pray to God. If they don't believe in God, then why are they offended?

> *Woe to those who call evil good, and good evil;*
>
> *Who put darkness for light, and light for darkness;*
>
> *Who put bitter for sweet, and sweet for bitter!*
>
> —*ISAIAH 5:20 (NKJV)*

The whole world does this today. They promote sinful lifestyles, adult movies, lotteries, gambling, casinos, raffle tickets—all fueled by greed. What does God think about this? He told me it was *ill*-gotten gains. This is an improper way to receive money. Gambling casinos are built with the money that people lose. *The Bible* says after death comes your judgment.

> *Just as people are destined to die once, and after that to face judgment,*
>
> *so Christ was sacrificed once to take away the sins of many; and he will appear a second time, not to bear sin, but to bring salvation to those who are waiting for him.*
>
> *—HEBREWS 9:27 (NIV)*

> *Or do you not know that wrongdoers will not inherit the kingdom of God? Do not be deceived: Neither the sexually immoral nor idolaters nor adulterers nor men who have sex with men*
>
> *nor thieves nor the greedy nor drunkards nor slanderers nor swindlers will inherit the kingdom of God.*
>
> *—1 CORINTHIANS 6:9-10 (NIV)*

TRUE AND FALSE DISCIPLES

> *"Not everyone who says to me, 'Lord, Lord,' will enter the kingdom of heaven, but only the one who does the will of my Father who is in heaven.*

> *Many will say to me on that day, 'Lord, Lord, did we not prophesy in your name and in your name drive out demons and in your name perform many miracles?'*
>
> *Then I will tell them plainly, 'I never knew you. Away from me, you evildoers!'*
>
> *—MATTHEW 7:21-23 NIV*

> *He replied, 'Isaiah was right when he prophesied about you hypocrites; as it is written: "These people honor me with their lips, but their hearts are far from me.*
>
> *They worship me in vain; their teachings are merely human rules.'*
>
> *—MARK 7:6-7 (NIV)*

There are world religions that don't use *The Bible,* but have written their own books to live by. They are deceived by the devil, believing and living a lie. There are religions that teach it's okay to kill. Satan and his workers are here to steal, kill, and destroy. *The Bible* says that you will believe a lie and be damned by that lie.

> *. . . and all the ways that wickedness deceives those who are perishing. They perish because they refused to love the truth and so be saved.*

> *For this reason God sends them a powerful delusion so that they will believe the lie*
>
> *and so that all will be condemned who have not believed the truth but have delighted in wickedness.*
>
> *—2 THESSALONIANS 2:10-12 (NIV)*

The Bible is the written word of God, and Jesus is the truth. We have choices every day. We can choose to look every day at what we can get, or we can forget looking at truth and what God wants our choices to be. God wants our choices to line up with his word, *The Bible*. Blessings come from obeying god.

Because all have sinned, all can be forgiven in Christ. Everyone can be a servant in the body of Christ. Don't ever let your past determine your future. All Christians are sinners that have been forgiven. Join the family of God today. Ask Jesus to forgive you of your sins. Put your belief and trust in him. Make Jesus your Savior. Get water-baptized. Go to a Christian church that honors Jesus. Read your *Bible,* God's roadmap for your life. Remember, Satan will bring up your past to you; just tell him all your sins are under the blood of Jesus.

CHAPTER 4
Satan is Man's Enemy

Satan hates all humans because God created us and loves us. Read the following story of a righteous man who loved and honored God and what Satan (the devil) did to Job.

There was a man in the land of Uz whose name was Job. That man was without blame. He was right and good, he feared God, and turned away from sin.

Seven sons and three daughters were born to him.

He had 7,000 sheep, 3,000 camels, 1,000 oxen, 500 female donkeys, and many servants. He was the greatest of all the men of the east.

His sons used to go and make a special supper in each one's house on a special day. And they would send for their three sisters to eat and drink with them.

When the days of their special supper were over, Job would get up early in the morning and send for them. Then he would give burnt gifts for each of them so that they would be pure. For Job said, "It might be that my sons have sinned and cursed God in their hearts." Job always did this.

—JOB 1:1-5 (NIV)

JOB'S FIRST TEST

Now there was a day when the sons of God came to show themselves before the Lord. Satan came with them also.

And the Lord said to Satan, "Where have you come from?" Satan answered the Lord and said, "From traveling around on the earth and walking around on it."

The Lord said to Satan, "Have you thought about My servant Job? For there is no one like him on the earth. He is without blame, a man who is right and good. He honors God with fear and turns away from sin."

Then Satan answered the Lord, "Does Job fear God for nothing?

Have You not made a wall around him and his house and all that he has, on every side? You have brought good to the work of his hands, and he has received more and more in the land.

But put out Your hand now and touch all that he has. And for sure he will curse You to Your face."

Then the Lord said to Satan, "See, all that he has is in your power. Only do not put your hand on him." So, Satan went out from the Lord.

On a day when Job's sons and daughters were eating and drinking wine in their oldest brother's house,

a man came to Job with news, saying, "The oxen were pulling the plow and the donkeys were eating beside them.

And the Sabeans came and took them. They also killed the servants with the sword. I alone have run away from them to tell you."

While he was still speaking, another man came and said, "The fire of God fell from heaven and burned up the sheep and the servants and destroyed them. I alone have gotten away to tell you."

While he was still speaking, another came and said, "The Babylonians divided into three groups and came to fight. They took the camels and killed the servants with the sword. I alone have gotten away to tell you."

While he was still speaking, another also came and said, "Your sons and daughters were eating and drinking wine in their oldest brother's house.

And see, a strong wind came from the desert and hit the four corners of the house. It fell on the young people and they are dead. I alone have gotten away to tell you."

Then Job stood up and tore his clothing and cut the hair from his head. And he fell to the ground and worshiped.

He said, "Without clothing I was born from my mother, and without clothing I will return. The Lord gave and the Lord has taken away. Praise the name of the Lord."

In all this Job did not sin or blame God.

—JOB 1:6-22 (NLT)

JOB'S SECOND TEST

One day the members of the heavenly court came again to present themselves before the LORD, *and the Accuser, Satan, came with them. "Where have you come from?" the* LORD *asked Satan.*

Satan answered the LORD, *"I have been patrolling the earth, watching everything that's going on."*

Then the LORD *asked Satan, "Have you noticed my servant Job? He is the finest man in all the earth. He is blameless—a man of complete integrity. He fears God and stays away from evil. And he has maintained his integrity, even though you urged me to harm him without cause."*

Satan replied to the LORD, *"Skin for skin! A man will give up everything he has to save his life. But reach out and take away his health, and he will surely curse you to your face!"*

"All right, do with him as you please," the LORD said to Satan. "But spare his life." So Satan left the LORD's presence, and he struck Job with terrible boils from head to foot.

Job scraped his skin with a piece of broken pottery as he sat among the ashes. His wife said to him, "Are you still trying to maintain your integrity? Curse God and die."

But Job replied, "You talk like a foolish woman. Should we accept only good things from the hand of God and never anything bad?" So in all this, Job said nothing wrong.

—JOB 2:1-10 (NLT)

Satan is behind all sickness and disease. Satan desires to get people to be mad at God and blame God for something he knows he is behind. He delights in this. I know of a man who said he would never serve God because his wife wasn't healed of cancer. He blamed God. Satan was behind her sickness. Job never got mad at God or spoke a word against God. We will never have all the answers why God allows things to happen to people but only God knows why. God's ways are always good and he knows what's best and wants only the best for us.

> *"For my thoughts are not your thoughts, neither are your ways my ways," declares the* LORD.
>
> *"As the heavens are higher than the earth, so are my ways higher than your ways and my thoughts than your thoughts.*
>
> —ISAIAH 55:8-9 (NIV)

Evil is here on earth so things will always happen. *The Bible* says that Satan is the evil ruler of the whole world. Satan is described in *The Bible* as a murderer. The devil was called a serpent when he deceived Eve and Adam to disobey God and brought sin into the world. Other names include the evil one, the destroyer, the liar, the hater of good. These are just a few of the titles that are given to the devil. Humans invite Satan the devil into their lives by the choices they make. *Satan is here to steal, kill, and destroy!*

> *The thief comes only to steal and kill and destroy; I have come that they may have life, and have it to the full.*
>
> —JOHN 10:10 (NIV)

Alcoholics start out by having one drink, and then alcohol gets a hook in them. Alcohol destroys the person and the family. It steals everything from them. The bottle becomes their best friend, and they will do anything to get that drink.

People today want to legalize marijuana. I have known people who started out with marijuana, then went to cocaine, and they got hooked on it and spent all their money to buy it. They had no money left to provide for their family. People have killed others just to get money for cocaine. Our prisons are filled with people who have committed crimes under the influence of alcohol and drugs. Our prison systems are costing taxpayers billions of dollars a year to operate.

Women get pregnant and in desperation have an abortion that ends the baby's life. The devil entices you to have an abortion and then condemns you and torments you for having it. By asking Jesus to come into your life there is forgiveness and a new start in life.

People play the lottery and go to gambling casinos all in the name of greed. The casinos are built and ran on the loser's money. People get hooked on gambling. There is more money given to the states and less money for you. A lot of families have been destroyed because of gambling.

Pornography has affected both men and women, destroying marriages, breaking families apart. It causes men to rape women. It causes affairs between both sexes. It brings billions of dollars into the people that produce pornography. It causes children to be molested. Many rapists have admitted that they have started out with pornography. Sin doesn't pay, but there is a price to pay with sin. A forest fire starts with a small spark. "Just one peek at an adult magazine won't hurt. Just one adult movie between us for entertainment with our marriage will help spice up our marriage."

If you play with fire you will get burnt. These sayings are an open door for destruction with Satan hiding behind that door. The deeper you go into sin, the more Satan pushes you. Satan is behind all sin. What is sin? Sin is anything in violation of God's perfect will for all mankind.

Satan likes to blind the eyes and ears of people so they won't believe *The Bible* and come to Jesus. Reading God's word, *The Bible,* gives you knowledge of who Jesus is, and following Jesus is your entrance into heaven.

Satan uses his family of demons to bring warfare against people, especially Christians. When I came back to the Lord the second time, I had a powerful attack from demons attacking my mind. I had no rest day or night from these filthy thoughts about Jesus. This went on for months. I went to a pastor who told me I was demon-possessed. He prayed for me and said he cast thirteen demons out of me. He said if I didn't come to his church, the demons would come back into me.

The next morning the thoughts were still there. I went to another pastor and told him of the thoughts I was having. He told me about another man two weeks prior to my visit who had the same thoughts I had. He asked me if I loved the blood of Jesus, and I answered, "I do love the blood of Jesus. Jesus's blood cleanses us from all sin." This pastor assured me I was not demon-possessed. He said every time those thoughts come into my mind, just say, "I love the blood of Jesus."

I went home with those thoughts still in my mind and did as he said. I would repeat over and over, "I love the blood of Jesus," and these thoughts continued for some time. I did not stop saying, "I love the blood of Jesus," and finally these demonic thoughts left me. God then spoke to my heart and told me that those thoughts were put there by the devil.

When I was a kid my grandfather, Hallie Davis, told me about his aunt who would pray to Satan. He said that he saw her through her practice of Satanism to cause a piano to rise off the floor. One night when she was in bed something started hitting her with a whip. She became so frightened she stopped her practice of Satanism. She would never tell anyone the words she said to Satan.

I knew of another person who played with the demonic world. She read books on witchcraft and prayed to Satan. She told me that she saw a window open by itself. Opening herself up to Satan has caused her to have a lot of mental problems. When you play with Ouija boards, tarot cards, crystal balls, black magic, or praying to the dead, you are inviting the demonic into your life.

My sister Shirley rented a house in Michigan. I went into her basement to get something. I heard something growl at me. I knew it was demonic. It didn't take me long to get out of that basement. Later on, I asked my sister if anything weird had happened to her in that house. She said weird, yes, and she began to tell me that she was in bed and heard something in the basement bouncing a ball. She said she went down to the basement and there was no ball down there. She told me one night she went to bed and something was under her bed pushing up hard and fast on her mattress. She said she got up and looked under her bed, but nothing was there. My sister had her grandkids over for the weekend. She took them home, then came back and made the bed. She had gone into the bedroom many times during the week. She came home from work, went into the bedroom, and the radio was playing. She told me of other things that happened in that demonic house.

JESUS CASTS OUT A DEMON

Then Jesus went to Capernaum, a town in Galilee, and taught there in the synagogue every Sabbath day.

There, too, the people were amazed at his teaching, for he spoke with authority.

Once when he was in the synagogue, a man possessed by a demon—an evil spirit—began shouting at Jesus,

"Go away! Why are you interfering with us, Jesus of Nazareth? Have you come to destroy us? I know who you are—the Holy One of God!"

Jesus cut him short. "Be quiet! Come out of the man," he ordered. At that, the demon threw the man to the floor as the crowd watched; then it came out of him without hurting him further.

Amazed, the people exclaimed, "What authority and power this man's words possess! Even evil spirits obey him, and they flee at his command!"

The news about Jesus spread through every village in the entire region.

—LUKE 4:31-37 (NLT)

Demons are evil Spirts of Satan who want to possess people. Demons are as real today as they were back in the days when Jesus was on the earth.

JESUS HEALS A DEMON-POSSESSED MAN

So they arrived at the other side of the lake, in the region of the Gerasenes.

When Jesus climbed out of the boat, a man possessed by an evil spirit came out from a cemetery to meet him.

This man lived among the burial caves and could no longer be restrained, even with a chain.

Whenever he was put into chains and shackles—as he often was—he snapped the chains from his wrists and smashed the shackles. No one was strong enough to subdue him.

Day and night he wandered among the burial caves and in the hills, howling and cutting himself with sharp stones.

When Jesus was still some distance away, the man saw him, ran to meet him, and bowed low before him.

With a shriek, he screamed, "Why are you interfering with me, Jesus, Son of the Most High God? In the name of God, I beg you, don't torture me!"

For Jesus had already said to the spirit, "Come out of the man, you evil spirit."

Then Jesus demanded, "What is your name?"

And he replied, "My name is Legion, because there are many of us inside this man."

Then the evil spirits begged him again and again not to send them to some distant place.

There happened to be a large herd of pigs feeding on the hillside nearby.

"Send us into those pigs," the spirits begged. "Let us enter them."

So Jesus gave them permission. The evil spirits came out of the man and entered the pigs, and the entire herd of about 2,000 pigs plunged down the steep hillside into the lake and drowned in the water.

The herdsmen fled to the nearby town and the surrounding countryside, spreading the news as they ran. People rushed out to see what had happened.

A crowd soon gathered around Jesus, and they saw the man who had been possessed by the legion of demons. He was sitting there fully clothed and perfectly sane, and they were all afraid.

Then those who had seen what happened told the others about the demon-possessed man and the pigs.

And the crowd began pleading with Jesus to go away and leave them alone.

As Jesus was getting into the boat, the man who had been demon possessed begged to go with him.

But Jesus said, "No, go home to your family, and tell them everything the Lord has done for you and how merciful he has been."

So the man started off to visit the Ten Towns of that region and began to proclaim the great things Jesus had done for him; and everyone was amazed at what he told them.

—MARK 5:1-18 (NLT)

Satan can defeat you with mindsets on how you view God and what you think about him.

Do you see God as your loving father? (Psalms 103:13)

Do you see God as your shepherd? (Psalms 23:1 and Isaiah 40:11)

Do you see God as all powerful? (Jeremiah 10:6)

Do you see God as your Prince of Peace? (Isaiah 9:6 and John 14:27)

Do you see God as your helper? (Isaiah 41:10 and Psalms 121:2)

Do you see God as tender and filled with compassion toward you? (Psalm 103:8)

Do you see God as kind? (Psalm 145:7)

Do you see God as cruel, evil, unkind, angered at you, hating you, uncaring? DO you blame him for all your problems? *Now you're viewing God the way your enemy the devil wants you to see Him. The truth is God is a loving, kind, caring, and forgiving Father to all. Satan is cruel, unkind, and evil—filled with hate. He is a liar and a murderer. He loves to destroy people's lives and bring shame and condemnation on people.*

CHAPTER 5
SATAN FOCUSES ON OUR WEAKNESS

THE WHOLE ARMOR OF GOD

A final word: Be strong in the Lord and in his mighty power.

Put on all of God's armor so that you will be able to stand firm against all strategies of the devil.

For we are not fighting against flesh-and-blood enemies, but against evil rulers and authorities of the unseen world, against mighty powers in this dark world, and against evil spirits in the heavenly places.

Therefore, put on every piece of God's armor so you will be able to resist the enemy in the time of evil. Then after the battle you will still be standing firm.

Stand your ground, putting on the belt of truth and the body armor of God's righteousness.

For shoes, put on the peace that comes from the Good News so that you will be fully prepared.

In addition to all of these, hold up the shield of faith to stop the fiery arrows of the devil.

Put on salvation as your helmet, and take the sword of the Spirit, which is the word of God.

—EPHESIANS CHAPTER 6:10-17 (NLT)

What are the weaknesses of people that Satan uses?

One thing people struggle with is fear. Jesus said over and over fear not but have faith. There are so many things that people fear: fear of flying, fear of heights, fear of dying, fear of the dark, fear of people, fear of tight places, fear of commitment or marriage, fear to start a new job, fear of failure.

FLYING

I had a family member who had a fear of flying. She was forced to fly because of circumstances. After she faced her fear and flew, all she talked about is how much she loved flying.

FEAR OF PEOPLE

Every day you meet people who have been so hurt by the people around them that they put up walls and are afraid to let anyone close. Being hurt by a friend in the past, or having a spouse reject you can leave you wounded. People say things that can make you feel rejected, such as, "Let's have coffee sometime" when you know they do not intend to do it. You say, "It is so nice to see you," when you did not know what else to say and couldn't wait to get away. Later those who have promised you they would call and never do leave you with the idea that you are not important to them.

FEAR OF FAILURE

Many people who became successful had a lot of failures but never quit. Thomas Edison failed many times, trying to invent the light bulb. Colonel Sanders's Kentucky Fried Chicken, the Wright brothers making the airplane, and many more can be listed. Quitting is the only way to failure.

If you have fears, don't let that stop you from enjoying your life. *Do it afraid.* With every fear, there is bondage.

LACK OF CONFIDENCE

I had a stepfather when I was a child. I would ask him for a wrench to fix my bike. He always went to the tool box where I was and took the tool from my hand and fixed my bike himself. Then he said, "Lannie, you can't do anything. You are dumb. What are you going to do when I am gone?" It totally took my confidence and affected me all through my childhood. I felt dumb.

When I became a young man and started working in a factory, I had no confidence in my ability to do the job. I had so much fear of failure, all because of my stepfather's words. He did the same thing to my sister, and she talked about how it affected her and she said she felt dumb. As I look back I realize my stepfather did not have confidence, so he gained confidence through putting me down. Negative words can really cause harm and damage to people for life if they continue to believe them. That's why God warns us about the words we use. Be careful of what you say to your children. The truth is, *Sticks and stones can break my bones, but your words can destroy people.*

When I was young I use to hear words like, "You ought to be ashamed of yourself" for any wrong that I may have done. When I went down to a friend's house three days in a row, I was told I was making a pest out of myself and wearing out my welcome. I would hear, "Lannie, don't you think those people get tired of you coming to their house?" I started to feel no one liked me. This affected me for years. If someone came over to see me, I was told they were using me for my car or my money. Most times that I asked my mother for money or anything else, I was told no. I heard *No!* so much, I quit asking for anything. I would make it on my own, and I did. I found ways to make money. Those words really caused me to have wrong mindsets. I still struggle with those words I heard for so many years.

> *The tongue can bring death or life; those who love to talk will reap the consequences.*
> —PROVERBS 18:21 (NLT)

In Genesis chapter one God created all things by speaking words from his mouth.

Watch what you say! Once you speak it you can never take it back.

> *An offended friend is harder to win back than a fortified city. Arguments separate friends like a gate locked with bars.*
>
> —PROVERBS 18:19 (NLT)

Have you ever had someone say something to you that hurt you deeply and you had trouble forgetting their words?

When I was younger I took a ministry training class. I was required to give a three-to-five-minute sermon. All the people of the class would grade you how you did after your speech. The teacher graded me well. I looked at the sheets that the students filled out and all but one had excellent speech and great comments. One lady that was always negative wrote it was the worst message she ever heard in her life. I had the most trouble forgetting that negative comment. Now I am much older and wiser, and I don't try to let people who are negative affect me. It's not easy to deal with people who offend you. It is like a bulldozer running over you; it pushes you down. Words affect us. Words have caused people to commit suicide. Use your words to build up people, not tear them down.

When God has placed a dream in your heart, and if you share it with other people, they won't always agree with you. I have had things God has put into my heart, and some people have told me that God would never use me because I have been divorced. Some People told Joyce Meyer, a great *Bible* teacher, that God would never use her because she was a woman. Dave and Joyce Meyer have one of the largest ministries in the world. We watch her daily on television, and she is definitely called by God. Thank God that Joyce followed God and not her friends.

Nothing will get you more off track with your God-given dreams than how you think. God says that all things are possible with him. Believe what God has told you, and then do it. Be a winner, not a loser. With God, his promises are *Yes* and *Amen*. Believe and receive! Doubt and pout.

SATAN USES THE SELFISHNESS OF MAN

When my wife was growing up, she had a family member who had no thought of anything but her friends. She had an appointment book she took out to see where she could schedule us in for a visit. She was influenced by her so-called friends. Her whole life was a social circle. She had very little time for family. When she got older, she quickly realized she had no true friends.

She said to us, "Where are all my friends?" This family member listened to people. She did not pay attention to

God and what he wanted for her life. Her dream was social events and friends. Yes, she went to church and had social tea parties regularly. She listened to all the words her friends said and followed all the things they did. In the end, she died sad, crying for her friends. Satan wants us out of balance with the focus being about what we want. My family member wanted friends but she had no time for God outside of church.

I knew a woman who told me her life story. She was married and had one child. Her daughter lived away from Lansing. This friend and her husband went camping every weekend. They were happy together and wanted no friends. People approached them and wanted to become friends. They both let people know they were not interested in any friends. One weekend her husband had a sore throat. He had throat cancer with a short time to live. After he died, she told me that because of their selfishness, she didn't drive, and she had no friends to help her. She had no one in Lansing to help her. She regretted not making friends. I helped her until she moved away to be with her daughter. God wants us to have balance in our lives.

Solomon was the wisest man in history. Solomon disobeyed God by marrying foreign women who served false Gods. God was not saying he could not marry women, for he could marry as many women as he wanted within the boundary that God set for him. Solomon knew right from wrong, and he knew exactly the boundary where he was to not marry women because they served other Gods. Solomon decided that he wanted all the women he could get, regardless of which God they served. He was getting his eyes off God and getting his eyes on his desire, acting in selfishness. Solomon began looking away from God and looking at women, to what they wanted. Solomon loved to do for women like build false Gods for them to worship. Solomon then began to worship these false God's himself. Any time a person disobeys God, that leads to sin.

> *Draw near to God and He will draw near to you. Cleanse your hands, you sinners; and purify your hearts, you double-minded.*
>
> *—JAMES 4:8 (NKJV)*

> *So he answered and said, "'You shall love the LORD your God with all your heart, with all your soul, with all your strength, and with your entire mind,' and 'your neighbor as yourself.'"*
>
> *—LUKE 10:27 (NKJV)*

To love the Lord is to put God first in your daily life. That is to start each day off with God. To some people, their God is the television. Some have social media as their

God. God will not compete with any of these things. Some men claim they love God, but they live their lives for sports. There is nothing wrong with any of these things as long as God has first place. Anything that you put ahead of God is an idol in your life. God wants first place or no place.

> *I know what you are doing. You are not cold or hot. I wish you were one or the other.*
>
> *But because you are warm, and not hot or cold, I will spit you out of my mouth.*
>
> —REVELATION 3:15-16 (NLV)

God will not ride in the backseat of your life. These are people God was talking to about being warm. These people didn't please God. Have you ever had a friend who was lukewarm towards you? You can't call him a true friend. I have had a few lukewarm friends I couldn't rely on or depend upon. Judas Iscariot was one of the chosen disciples, but he put his love for money first, and he betrayed Jesus.

We have an enemy that hates God and hates you. Satan hates it when we put God first; however, God loves being first in our life. God deserves first place.

SATAN'S FAMILY

Let me introduce them to you. His first cousin is marijuana. He makes you feel so high, but after time he can't satisfy, so you go deeper into Satan's family. You meet his cousin cocaine. He makes you feel really good. After one time he has got you! Then you will find you will do anything to get money to buy and have cocaine. People will lie, steal, rob, and kill to get cocaine. Prisons are filled with people who got hooked on cocaine. There is also a cousin called Heroin. He will drive you crazy and make you violent. You won't know what you are doing. You must have heroin. One date with him and you will never be the same. Your family and friends will disown you. You won't be able to keep a job. Your life will be controlled by heroin. A woman will sell her body for drugs. Drugs will alter your brain forever.

Let me introduce you to Satan's cousin called sex. *Feels so good!* Sexual affairs or one-night stands can destroy you. It can break your home up and bring shame to you, maybe give you a disease or a pregnancy. Satan tells you to have an abortion, then he condemns you. You killed your baby. I know a woman who had an affair on her husband. She lost him and her kids. She had a mental breakdown. He never took her back.

Pornography destroys men and women. People look at each other as a cheap thrill. Hollywood gets rich with pornography.

Let me introduce you to another of his cousins: alcohol. I have seen this one big-time in men and women. Alcoholics all have the same friend and are loyal to the bottle. They will lie, steal, and do anything to get the bottle. The bottle comes before their family. Most can't hold a job. It takes all their money. They can't make it through a day without their bottle. It totally brings good people down, destroys marriages, and creates fights and arguments. A drunken mom or dad puts fear in their children when they see them drunk.

There is a cousin of fun called gambling. Casinos are built by losers. The devil whispers to you: "Try again, you may win." The result is you lose all your food money, your house, and your marriage. This is Satan's family. Their last name is *The Destroyers!* Their nickname is "We got you." Satan is here to steal, kill, and destroy. Satan never sleeps. He is always working to destroy God's plans for your life. People must learn God's Word the *Bible* for themselves. Jesus used the Word to fight against Satan when he was here on earth. Satan is totally evil. There is no good thing in him. Sin may be fun for a while, but in the end it will bring destruction to a person's life.

CHAPTER 6
JESUS

Who is Jesus? Jesus is God's son; and all that God is, Jesus is. Jesus was with his father God when he created all mankind.

> *And God said, Let us make man in our image, after our likeness:*

—GENESIS 1:26 (KJV)

Jesus was here from the beginning and has always existed. He came to earth from heaven. His home is in heaven. Why is Jesus the only way into heaven? He is God's Son, and he created all of mankind. In fact, everything that is here, Jesus created with his Father and the Holy Spirit. He shed his holy blood for the sins of the whole world: yours and mine.

> *For God so loved the world that he gave his only begotten Son, that whosoever believeth in him should not perish, but have everlasting life.*
>
> *For God sent not his Son into the world to condemn the world; but that the world through him might be saved.*
>
> *He that believeth on him is not condemned: but he that believeth not is condemned already, because he hath not believed in the name of the only begotten Son of God.*
>
> *—JOHN 3:16-18 (KJV)*

I thought one day of all the things Jesus has done—not the things he has done just for others, but for me as well. I said, "Jesus, what can I do to repay you for all you've done for me?"

I said, "I can't buy you a car because you won't drive it. I can't make you a cake because you won't eat it. What can I do for you, Jesus?

He spoke to me and said, "Feed my sheep." God wants us to help and give and care for all born again Christians.

The Father loveth the Son, and hath given all things into his hand.

He that believeth on the Son hath everlasting life: and he that believeth not the Son shall not see life; but the wrath of God abideth on him.

—JOHN 3:35-36 (KJV)

And Jesus came and spake unto them, saying, All power is given unto me in heaven and in earth.

Go ye therefore, and teach all nations, baptizing them in the name of the Father, and of the Son, and of the Holy Ghost:

Teaching them to observe all things whatsoever I have commanded you: and, lo, I am with you always, even unto the end of the world. Amen.

—MATTHEW 28:18-20 (KJV)

I am he that liveth, and was dead; and, behold, I am alive for evermore, Amen; and have the keys of hell and of death.

—REVELATION 1:18 (KJV)

Jesus has the power over Satan and demons. Jesus is the King of kings and Lord of lords. Jesus is ahead of all and is everything.

For all have sinned, and come short of the glory of God;

—*Romans 3:23 (KJV)*

So then, since we have a great High Priest who has entered heaven, Jesus the Son of God, let us hold firmly to what we believe.

This High Priest of ours understands our weaknesses, for he faced all of the same testings' we do, yet he did not sin.

So let us come boldly to the throne of our gracious God. There we will receive his mercy, and we will find grace to help us when we need it most.

—*HEBREWS 4:14-16 (NLT)*

This high priest of ours understands our weaknesses, for he faced all of the same testings we do, yet he did not sin.

Jesus is a wonderful Lord and Savior; he really loves you. Read the whole book of John in *The Bible*. Go to the New Testament and you will find it after the book of Luke. Make Jesus your best friend by asking him into your heart and life. Jesus will be your best friend you will ever have.

THE HOLY SPIRIT

But the Helper, the Holy Spirit, whom the Father will send in My name, He will teach you all things, and bring to your remembrance all things that I said to you.

—*JOHN 14:26 (NKJV)*

The Holy Spirit is our helper. He lives inside of the Christian. He convicts people of sin. The Holy Spirit is not on the inside of non-Christians, but he is constantly trying to draw all people to Jesus. The non-Christian is not aware of the Holy Spirit, but that does not stop him from working. The Holy Spirit is the third person of the godhead, the Father God, Jesus his son, and the Holy Spirit. The Holy Spirit produces this kind of fruit in our lives.

> *But the Holy Spirit produces this kind of fruit in our lives: love, joy, peace, patience, kindness, goodness, faithfulness, gentleness, and self-control. There is no law against these things!*
>
> —GALATIANS 5:22-23 (NLT)

The Holy Spirit is always loving and never condemning to us. He gives joy and peace even in the midst of a painful situation. He is patient with us. As he speaks the truth to us, he is always pouring out kindness and goodness, being faithful and gentle and always doing and saying the right things. Truth teaches us and will always lead us and help us. The scripture above, John 14:26, tells us he is our teacher.

THE PRAYER FOR SALVATION

Jesus,

I confess my sins. I am a sinner. I need a Savior. I believe you died on the cross for me. Forgive me of all my sins and wash me clean. Come into my heart and be Lord of my life. Amen.

SALVATION

1. John 3:3-6 We must be born again.

2. 2 Corinthians 5:17-21 We become new creatures.

3. Romans 10:9-10 This teaches how to receive.

4. Acts 2:21 Whoever calls on him will be saved.

5. John 3:16-18 God so loved the world he gave his son.

6. Ephesians 2:8 Salvation is a free gift.

7. Revelation 3:20 God knocks.

If you said this prayer and meant it, you are now born again. Get water-baptized. Read *The Bible* daily. Go to a Christian church where Jesus is preached and honored as Lord. Love God and love others. God loves you—yes, you—just as you are.

Warning!
No One Is Scared of Hell
Until They Get There!
It's a real place, and you need to know the truth before you die.

I hope you're not like so many people who go through life wanting more and more. People get caught up in living life, never giving a thought to eternity. Everyone will eventually die and find out the truth about what happens after death. God created the soul, which is who we are. Our life is inside our body. The body is only our carrying case for us on this earth. Our soul never dies. Read this book before it's too late for you.

Print & Ebook Editions from The Fresh Ink Group

The Fresh Ink Group

Publishing
Free Memberships
Free Stories, Essays, Articles
Free-Story Newsletter
Writing Contests

Books
Ebooks
Amazon Bookstore

Authors
Editors
Artists
Professionals
Publishing Services
Publisher Resources

Readers' Forum
Blogs
Social Media

www.FreshInkGroup.com
Email: info@FreshInkGroup.com

www.ingramcontent.com/pod-product-compliance
Lightning Source LLC
Chambersburg PA
CBHW021444080526
44588CB00009B/682